You Dreamed of Being a Veterinarian?

Dr. Kristina Kiefer

BookLeaf Publishing

India | USA | UK

You Dreamed of Being a Veterinarian? ©
2024 Dr. Kristina Kiefer

Presentation by *BookLeaf Publishing*

Web: www.bookleafpub.com

E-mail: info@bookleafpub.com

ISBN: 9789358317558

First edition 2024

DEDICATION

To the pets I have the honor of helping, the people that trust me with their best friends, and the souls that have supported me every step of this journey.

Graveyard

There is a graveyard next to work.
Lucky bastards in it get an enviable perk.
Sleep. When I leave they are all asleep.
Soft solar lights shadow gravestones, but not a
peep.
Three bites into 10pm dinner.
My hopes shattered by the intrusive ringer.

The graveyard shift has a question.
"When there's intestines outside someone else's
spay incision…?"
"It's an emergency." But it progresses otherwise.

Approval, paperwork, assemble team: a
complicated enterprise.
The body demands rest, the mind has begun a
marathon—
Knowing there is still work to be done.

The graveyard of my hopes and dreams gain
new occupants tonight,
As I begin tomorrow—-before today has even
been set right.
1:21 AM they call to come in,
My counting sheep not even at a stage to begin.

The lights are on in the graveyard office as I
drive by,
The open sign blinking in my sleepy eye.
Strange, because it's never been on—day or
night—before.
2:52 am before they are actually ready for me in
the OR,
Twenty one minutes to find no intestines. Makes
me edgy—
Six and half hours of sleep, stolen for
twenty-one minutes of me.

Too tired to remember to check if the graveyard
next door
Is still open for business in this dawn downpour.

Finally. Finally I can rest my body in its
graveyard of sleep.
Until two hours later, I rise again. Pray. My soul
to keep.

M'love

Two hours of sleep amidst thirty-six hours of
work,
I drag myself to the purveyor of caffeine, for a
tiny perk.
The barista greets me with a warm cup and
"Here ya are, m'love!"
I shock myself as tears flow hearing what her
greeting consists of.
The simple tenderness of a stranger,
Ringing an alarm for an unspoken danger.
My soul leaks as I ponder this thing that has
given me shivers:
Who takes care of the caregivers?!
Those who are long on strong, but short on
time?
Hearts whose contemplation is saved for
bedtime,
Yet find exhaustion claiming that theoretic
space.
The capacity to understand their own wants
finding no place.
Let alone communicating needs.
Evermore, demand increasing our speeds,
til something as simple as m'love cracks our
facade

hinting that maybe something is flawed.
If there isn't a loved one to bear witness,
it becomes a problem for another time, yet again
undermining our fitness.
Care of the caregiver is so easily neglected,
by those we need, but most especially by those
so deeply affected.

Recovery?

It's Saturday- after a five-day-work week.
"A day off"—let me give you a peak:
After seventy hours in five days: sleep in.
Except... only a couple hours, to my chagrin.
In hospital patients still need my care,
Even if my intern allows me to not be there.
Once they are squared away,
back in my bed I lay.
Trying to make up the rest I need to do it all
over.
But quite soon I hear the phone from beneath the
bedcover.
I'm needed for an emergency surgery,
the reserves I've gained only enough to avoid me
being ornery.
A second surgery awaits by my arrival.
Today, I accomplish nothing more than survival.

The Thing About Work Relationships

Sunday should be my fun day.
Even if in-hospital patients get a little in the
way.
Lack of sleep makes me slow to get out the door
but I ignore my to-do list to go wander around
the moor.
A delicate balance: life chores versus mental
restore—
many times the choice can't be "and", rather
strictly becomes "or".
A few hours to renew my nature, by visiting its
Mother.
Cutting it short to meet with another.
Two strangers with commonalities so strong the
conversation never stalls.
Yet inevitable, at some point discussion of our
work falls.
I bear witness to her frustrations—
the reasons for her burnout foundations.
Only two weeks back to clinics for her
and she sees so much that makes her wish to
defer
a commitment to persist
in the challenges no longer easily dismissed.

My heart feels her struggle.
Honored by trust but saddened with empathy is
always the juggle.
Nature may have been a balm,
but today this introvert has not been granted
calm.

Just a Day's Work

Save the dog that is limping—
There isn't a moment he's not gimping.
Meds haven't worked.
Family ignores instructions that he should be
inert.

Puppy in because she's outgrown her cast.
Four weeks ago was the last.
Full anesthesia so that she doesn't end up
paralyzed.
Too young even to be surgerized.
Full body cast is her lot in life,
though it seems to cause her no strife.

Another kiddo limping all day.
Her importance to mom is hard to convey.
Imagine your independence resting on paws.
Paws that have suddenly developed flaws.
Mom's eyes are on my surgery table.
Depending fully on me to make things stable.

This is bad—1 in 4 dogs don't make it home.
Necessary risk is our current zone.
Surgery proves it's worse than we thought.
Mom is distraught.
She weeps—my first human child arrives in
weeks—in order for them to meet I need her
alive!
But now we know 1 in 2 dogs won't survive.

This is only a day's work as a vet.
50% human, 50% pet.
The emotional jerk—
Just a day's work.

Paid to Pee

"My husband says my dog gets paid to pee."
Sounds like a lovely job to me—just a little wee!
No discussions over what is better: life or death.
No talking about how much it costs—just to
assess.
'Paid to Pee' sounds like a delightful gig!
Would it be silly at this point in my career to
renege?
Twelve years of college, five of specialized
training,
twenty-four years of practice—all of it draining.
I wonder what qualifications I need for the title
of 'Paid to Pee'?
For that matter, who would be responsible to
oversee?!
Applications and interviews all over again?!
I decide no, before the process even began.
Instead I'll choose to take a moment to delight,
in this owner's explanation for her overweight
girl's plight.

Do I Bother?

While walking the tri-pawed German shepherd
patient at night,
she begins to bark with all her might.
As a stranger boldly approaches.
"Be a good dog!" the person reproaches.

I am momentarily confused.
Do I bother to take the time to ensure the
stranger is disabused?

What makes a good dog?!
Is it a police dog that follows their genes to
sound the alarm?
Or the guard dog that makes a stranger feel
warm?

Watching the foot decay, day by day,
I recommend we amputate, without delay.
The owner weeps and protests,
"I cannot disable my dog!" she objects.

I am momentarily confused.
Do I bother to take the time to ensure the
stranger is disabused?

What makes a disabled dog?!
Is a disabled dog a rotting limb?
Or one less leg slim?

The owner asks for the gold standard care,
Having needed the same, they are fully aware.
The time, personnel, supplies and meticulous
skill,
Yet, given an estimate they become shrill.
"How can you talk about cost?!"
"You might not be the doctor for me, because
clearly your morals and heart are lost!"

I am momentarily confused.
Do I bother to take the time to ensure the
stranger is disabused?

What gives a doctor heart and sense?!
One with specialized staff, training, resources
facilities and a desire to offer top line care?
Or one that can't pay the bills, so is no longer
there?

Holiday Diseases

Every holiday has its own disease,
Things you can predict to see with increased
frequencies.

Halloween and Easter: chocolate toxicity.
Inattentive children and greedy doggos share
complicity.

Fourth of July: Hit by car.
The dogs get scared and try to run far.

Thanksgiving and Christmas may be the worst:
pancreatitis and euthanasias.
Too much rich food, family goodbyes and
monetary aplasias.

I found a new holiday disease here-
In Canada, the poppy pins of Remembrance Day
are something to fear!
Apparently they seem a tasty treat.
The number I've had to remove from stomachs
this week is an astonishing feat!

Another Loss

We lost another one today.
The number of colleagues that benefited from
him is hard to say.
Everyday he posted something to make us laugh.
Things relatable only to veterinary staff.
Thankfully, he made a choice that spares his life.
Thankfully, before surpassing his limit of strife.
Already trained and practicing as an electrician,
more money, less working and restored to
happiness, by his own admission.

We might lose another one today,
admitted for a hospital stay.
Finances, work stress, pet ownership disputes,
personal pet health—

all things that make them wish for their own
death.
1 in 6 of us has seriously considered suicide.
70% of us have experienced a colleague, who
chose this path and died.

Since my graduation—many years ago—
not a year passes without several who left us,
leaving another blow.
Many of us feel no judging or resentment—
rather we might start to wonder if it is the
answer to our own discontentment.

Saturday

17

Done with the clinic
Seventeen hours transit home
My own pets and bed

You're Fired

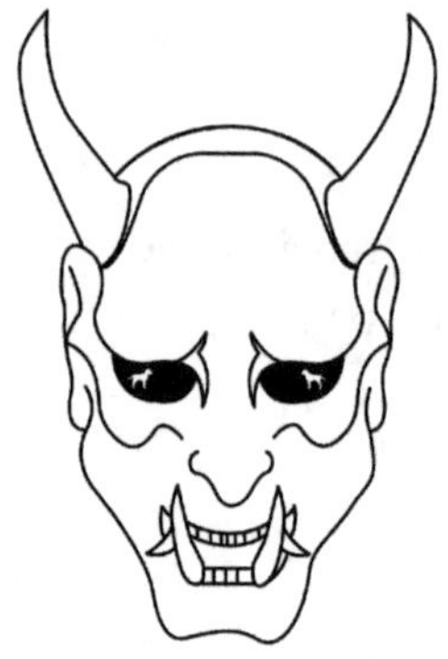

Today, one human made me hate them all.
I would love an emotional overhaul.
But instead their putridness has infected—
every positive moment from this week dejected.

They scream at my staff on the phone—
apologizing, yet still unleashing a tantrum—full
blown.
The surest way to raise my ire
is to mistreat the people I hire.

They were lucky I was hands deep in a body
cavity.
I have a way of making people face their own
depravity.
Which is a weapon to be used most cautiously,
but one I'm unsheathing at this moment with
glee.

You see, while you can fire someone you
employ,
it is also my prerogative to select only clients
who do not destroy joy!

I took a couple days in order to respond in
professionalism,
rather than fiery righteous activism,
my one day of rest in body only,
the mind wrestling with this task that is so
aggravating and lonely.

You are responsible for your behavior and its
undesirable consequences.
I, to ensure abuse of my staff is treated as the
most grievous of offenses.
Thus, it is my mixed pleasure to write to you
following the events transpired:
'Dear Mr. and/or Ms. so-and-so: YOU'RE
FIRED.

The Real Work Begins

What happens when I'm not scheduled in a
clinic?
I am an academic mimic.
I retain mountains of ceaseless work.
A cherished and intentional quirk.
More on the details later.
First order of business is to resurrect habits of
cultivation.
In the day's tasks I schedule a run.
Work has kept me from it so long that to start is
simply to want it done.
My hypocrisy is felt in mind, bone and ligament,
as I recall spending hours tending these tissues
in each and every patient.
Preaching against weekend warrior strategy,
yet letting my own muscles breakdown and
atrophy.
Too busy preaching to practice my own sound
advice,
with each footfall and joint strain I pay the price.
"Sweating is necessary for your mental
survival!"
The pain of body now versus mind on the
horizon is the formidable rival.

I struggle through creaky joints and willpower,
choosing to carry on in honor of the soul,
who used to run ten times more, but getting the
wheelchair out the door is her current goal.
Half the distance has fled before the weight
vanishes,
Joy, presence and recollection of love suddenly
banishes,
the should, must and obligation, as I recall this
forgotten passion.
Joy in journey, notice of nature, cold cheeks felt
as acts of self-compassion.
The feet return to fleet, in place of plodding.
Swollen stiff fingers refreshed and move
applauding,
as autumn leaves foreshadow snowflakes falling.
My heart reconnects with who I should be—this
run, an act of recalling.
I have not outrun the cumulative trauma of late.
But I have gained recognition of my current
state.
To be a veterinarian, stay a veterinarian, to
survive,
I should. Must. Need. Want. Long. Plead to run
to cling to being alive.

My Cat Says He Loves Me

No really. It's true.
I taught my cat to talk, not quite like me and
you.
He pushes buttons—Buttons with phrases on
them.
It truly challenges the perception that pets are
dumb.
It makes it that much harder to bear,
taking time from my cat, to give someone else's
care.
You'd think the pets of vets have it made,
yet emotional neglect is a hazard of this trade.
I taught him buttons over a year ago,
The "love you" button, only two days past
though.
Today he said "Love you",

and pierced my heart through.
What a wonder this creature is—
yet so often I place strangers' needs above his.
Who hears his "love you" button invite,
when I'm at the clinic from first light to
midnight?

Non-clinic Work

This week is a non-clinic week.
Here is just a little peak:
There is the mundane administration tasks:
Invoices, payments, renewals, license upkeep,
taxes.
There are the meetings:
Website designers, business strategy, service
building, prospective job greetings.
There is the community member contributions:
Peer reviewing articles, service puppy raising,
helping rescues find solutions.
There are projects for professional well-being:
Book Rounds, career longevity mentorship, grief
resource overseeing.
Even colleagues wonder how I fill my time
between visits,
forgetting the critical quality to achieve DVM:
ambitious.
There is more I want to do than I possibly can.
It would fill my entire lifespan.
There is so much more than puppies and kitties
all day,
if you dare to enter the fray!

Snerdle

My last day at home before off to the clinic I go,
the jumble of emotions makes quite a show.
With hefty enthuzimuzzy I hurkle-durkle to start
things right.
I've got the morbs, but a solid snerdle should fix
that plight,
my blanket made of poodle, husky and cat.
I'm sure you can mumble-cum-stumble that
the gigglemug of the poodle ensures
this lallygagging holds many allures.
"Flumgummery!" you may accuse me of,
but nanty narking and all other things I love,
are not your business, just my responsibility—
though I may be hufty-tufty in affability,
about the delights these creatures bring me,
given the hardship twelve days of separation
brings, I'm sure you'll agree.
"How dare you use phrases I do not know?"
You'll surely shout.

But medical terms and clients oft make
conversations like this, you'd quickly find out.
You get real good at researching all the things
that give you doubt,
so you avoid medical mistake fallout!
Enjoy these outdated phrases I learned,
while I enjoy the day of snerdle rest I earned!

Boundaries

A travel day to cover a clinic very far away
Twelve hours of my time, without pay.
I use the time for admin tasks,
when possible, as often the wi-fi lacks!
Halfway there and my phone rings,
not even there yet, and in a clinic problem
wings.
I don't resent the person with the questions or the
fears,
but it highlights the balance one must take with
peers.
Delicately teeter between support
And not cutting your mental needs short.
Boundaries, a source of jealousy or admiration
from some,
aggressive judgment and disparity from others
grown numb.

Not all can be helped, because some don't see
they are their own cripple.
You can only hope your intentional behavior has
a ripple.
In a profession which struggles to define
where responsibility should be released or
remain mine.
I can offer health and help for animals in my
care,
but only when owners choose to meet me there.
I can give energy and compassion,
but only within the limits of my ration.
Time, money, energy, focus—all come on a
budget.
And consequences begin to show when you
fudge it.
We are cultivated to take responsibility for the
whole world,
then get shocked when our suicide rates hurtle.
Certainly, the pressure of failure, real or owner
implied
plays a role, but rarely do we call out each
other's snide!
Overdrawing our account of compassion on
clients,
doesn't give you the right to bully colleagues
into compliance
with ways failing you
as those of us outside can view.

Your feelings of helplessness and frustrations
severely misdirected
towards those you should work hardest to ensure
are respected.
Our profession is riddled with a cancer,
yet so many of us outright reject the only
answer.
Setting, respecting and honoring boundaries as a
skill,
even in the face of those that meet them with
ill-will.
It's my decision whether or not I answer the ring,
when it comes to my boundaries, there is only
one king.

Listen Up

Blustery, chilly, gray day
to be out to play.
Stopped by a woman wandering,
asking for help in coffee conjuring.
Not having any change
I invited her to join me at a shop within our
range.
I couldn't talk her into lunch,
simply a muffin, because more was "too much".
She was profuse with gratitude,
her story after my prying an entire mood.
Forcibly removed from tent city,
her frustrations proved a model of gritty.
Social services cover a princely hotel nightly
fee,
four times my mortgage clear and free.
To keep her from the public eye,
and inadvertently, her relied upon supply:
shelter all times of day,
applications to achieve job pay,
soup kitchen access,
people that can direct recovery process.
Her voice chokes explaining since she got clean,
all the resources she was assured she was
morally owed became incredibly lean.

Every day became a much bigger fight,
matched with a backward slide in plight.
Her skillset a critical shortage in the nation,
but denied work due to red tape and bureaucratic
regulation.
The bitter irony being she could build the
housing she needs,
but obstruction to migrant licensure prohibiting
her from such deeds.
We part with hugs and tears,
her greatest gratitude being meeting someone
who cares.
"Thank you for taking the time to listen,"
she repeats a fourth time as her eyes continue to
glisten.
Another thing everyone failed to mention,
is that for clients, your most cherished skill is
your time and attention.
With corporatization and business courses,
time-management and efficiency have become
the predominant forces.
Yet, in diagnosis, clinic management and client
satisfaction,
listening and feeling heard gives by far the
greatest traction.
Absent in our selection criteria and coursework,
is that skill that is more than just a perk.
Acting as a social worker almost,

often what someone asks for isn't what matters foremost.
Turns out work isn't just fixing the pup—you'll avoid so much heartbreak and frustration if you learn to really, really listen up.

Be Prepared to Cry

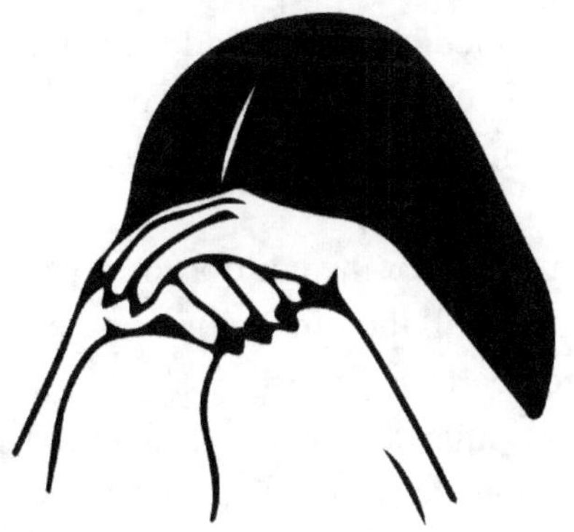

I watched an entire hospital infrastructure
crumble this week.
I gave a prognosis to a family today—it was less
than bleak.
I cried again.

I watched young interns' dreams evaporate
before their eyes.
A soul from a decade ago agreed to help with
speed which expectation denies.
I cried again.

A patient I did invasive surgery on leaps into my
arms for comfort and joy.
I saw someone extend way beyond duty at my
request—someone in my employ.
I cried again.

Something I did, did not go well. It may cost a
life.
Someone called me stupid and incapable
because they can't manage their own strife.
I cried again.

My heart aches for the comfort of my own pets
while I spend all the time helping others'
cherished hearts.
I was struck this day, by the amount of trust
given by clients as I practice my arts.
I cried again.

I learned of another colleague's heart, mind and
body broken by this profession, today.
A plea to another profession for a resource to
save an animal's life, brought two people gladly
out of their way.
I cried again.

There are no words that can prepare both the
tender heart and overwhelming level of
resilience you need to survive this job.
Rage. Heart sick. Joy. Honor. Fear.
Misunderstandings. Betrayal. Fulfilled lifelong
dreams. All have made me sob.
I cried again.

It's not for everyone, and many weeks I wonder
if I'd do it all once more.
But I have no regrets. Not even this crying
chore.
I cried again.

Hero to Zero

"You have given me so much comfort with this
decision; you are really good at your job."
says one client with a little relieved sob.

"It is complete incompetence that you did not do
what I told you to—it is REQUIRED!"
says the client that also documents exactly why
their request was incompetence—yet fails to see
how that misfired.

"I'm so grateful you were here when we needed
you most,"
says the client, who also brought us cookies
most grandiose.

"I am alarmed a surgeon didn't perform this! I
want to have a discussion about this
catastrophe!"
Newsflash—your ignorance is the
catastrophe—you are not a surgeon. I am. IT
WAS ME!

I get many, many more accolades than
denigrates.
Yet the negative echoes through my head and
never abates.
One moment a hero.
Many, many more, feeling like a zero.
I keep a book of all my thanks.
Because so often my purpose and reason tank.

Why Not Human Med?

Our student loans are the same.
There are miles between the tax brackets we
claim.
We both hold doctors of medicine.
They are licensed for the only species I am not,
whereas I am responsible for the health of your
pets, beef, pork and venison.
They choose a singular focus of disease.
Even as a specialist, I am responsible for all of
these.
They never get asked why they didn't decide to
be a "real doctor".
Guaranteed I will by every unfiltered talker.
They get titillated when we seek their input.
We are scandalized when their patients are
closer than a pole that is ten foot!
Our patients lick their butts.
Theirs shove things up them, like god-damned
wing nuts.
When I have to make pain to find it,
it's equally likely I'll get a kiss or get bit.
Their patients tell them where it hurts,
yet they still might get bit, which is infinitely
worse!

With my application I could have been one of
them three years earlier,
but am positive I would have ended up infinitely
surlier.
After the second vet school waitlist letter I
nearly went MD
but then and now, I am supremely confident it
wasn't for me!!!

Appreciation

It's heartbreaking how many feel appreciation of
their work is missing.
Finding pet owners, employers and colleagues in
the habit of dismissing.
How many of us put our heart and souls into
saving and improving other's life,
often to shocking levels of our own strife.
Imagine being the only veterinary surgeon for
almost 200,000 square miles.
Bearing the burden and numerous trials
of building a service in a remote corner of earth
That rivals the hospitals where humans might
have surgery or give birth.

For fifteen years you build and grow
rarely having time to lay low;
for patients arrive by car, plane or boat,
consuming every spare minute you devote.
"There is no one else who can do what you do!"
becomes an impossible burden when literal lives
are part of the milieux.
Then, the pandemic tripled the load.
No wonder well-being began to implode.
Finally-relief coverage to allow a few month
reprieve,
leaving it in the hands of a select few, who can
witness what you've managed to achieve.
They try to fill your shoes,
while from the incessant demands and pressure
you gift yourself recuse.
Over the months you wonder if you can persist,
and decide you can, but only with a partner to
enlist.
So you step back in the clinic role
and very quickly find so much changed away
from your original goal!
As you attempt to restore what seems undone,
the response seems calculated to stun.
"You just do the cutting.
We don't need you butting.
This thing you built—we'll manage it to the
hilt."
So you leave this monument of your own sweat.

The consequences they feel haven't even
achieved peak, yet.
I witness the start, middle, and end of this
conclusion,
there in the immediate confusion.
An impartial fill in
but the last surgeon of the season.
The anxiety is palpable from every corner,
for this temporary sojourner.
First, the employees strung along about
decisions regarding their fate.
Then me—wondering what becomes of my
patients if things don't go great!
Also the referring vet community,
upon learning there is no surgeon for three
months, who begin sneaking cases through ER
with impunity.
Would you, could you, tomorrow, since it's your
last day, fix this dog's non-life threatening knee?
What about the back of this walking dog, not in
any pain or dysfunction, but just because it's a
Frenchie?
This dog that has a lung mass, we knew about
months ago,
but surely you want to cut it before you go?
The hysteria, stress and load they've felt in a
decade,
putting on one last, great parade.

Neither they or you seeing the full value you brought.
Just me seeing as realization generates the overwrought.
No matter who you are: vet or not,
the absence of your presence is a vacuum fraught.
This heartbreaking story is true.
And I know many, many more than a few.
Ones who have changed jobs, professions or even planes of existence
When they have worn thin on resistance
Of the belief that the space would be better off without them
While the world tells them they are the sole factor for any outcome.
Be it a pet's life, employee's satisfaction or public perception of the profession,
the burden should never be just one person's to bear,
Especially not those that arrived here because they care.

In Conclusion

The moral of the story, if I may,
is to not underestimate the cost you will pay.
If you want to be a good vet,
a great owner to your pet,
an equal share member of your family,
someday, perhaps, you will want to be faculty,
or god-forbid, an active member of a
non-vet-med community,
maybe an engaged and joyful parent
(presumably)
or any of the other endless things you can be,
there will be a very steep fee.
Not just the debt of schooling—
which can be quite crippling,
but the work you'll need to survive,
and hopefully, eventually thrive.
The belief that you still matter,
in the face of colleague and client negative
batter.
The resilience and understanding that failure
is an inevitable and necessary component of the
road for an occasional savior.
That you need to get comfortable and intimately
know

that your most valuable and loving skill might
be to say no.
That you will need to be intentional about
thinking on the successes,
for they will rapidly be overwhelmed by the
stresses.
When you are done with vet school,
the easy part is done, as a general rule.
Now, you need to learn the intricacies
of managing yourself through the most
catastrophic of difficulties.
But if you dream of being a vet,
so that it burns your being more than any other
career you've met,
don't let other's regrets derail your goals,
but also don't neglect the lessons that trouble
their souls.
To see your dreams come true,
know that the hardest and never-ending work is
the care of you.
Go in, wide-eyes open,
with unwavering, uncompromising
self-supporting devotion.

A Note for My Veterinary Hopefuls

I have not solved the problem I face when an
eager student declares they want to be a vet. It's
a beautiful, wonderful and humbling profession.
But it will bring you to your knees, and it
literally kills some of us. A large number of
veterinarians feel it's their responsibility to
discourage people from choosing this
profession. Most of those vets wouldn't choose
it if given another chance. Even working in a
practice before applying to vet school doesn't
prepare you for the sudden burden of being
responsible. Responsible for the limitations of
your own humanity. Responsible for the actions
of everyone within your employ, or even anyone
who touches your patient. Responsible for life
and death advice. Responsible for massive debt.
Responsible for managing emotions—the vast
majority of which aren't even your own. The
burning desire to achieve this dream blinds us to
the suffering we will endure in perpetuity.
I haven't found a way to prepare veterinary
hopefuls for the reality, without discouraging the
brave souls meant to be alongside me in this
journey. I am one of the blessed veterinarians
that would choose this profession again, but I am
by no means happy every moment of the
journey. My hope is that you can use this book

to see the pain, beauty, frustration, unfairness,
potential, and joy and make the decision that is
right for you—but not without seeing the reality
of the existence you are choosing. I chose a
random day to start this book, as a challenge to
write a poem a day, and this is what the three
weeks following that day looked like. If you
choose clinical practice, you are likely to
encounter these feelings and situations, and
often. If you can still see the joy and value in the
work, come, join me. And bring your
therapist—we need them too!